Writing Builders

Seth and Savannah Build a

SPEECH

by Ann Ingalls
illustrated by Karen Lee

Content Consultant
Jan Lacina, Ph.D.
College of Education
Texas Christian University

Dedication: For my students

Norwood House Press
P.O. Box 316598
Chicago, Illinois 60631
For information regarding Norwood House Press, please visit
our website at:
www.norwoodhousepress.com or call 866-565-2900

Editor: Melissa York
Designer: Becky Daum
Project Management: Red Line Editorial

Library of Congress Cataloging-in-Publication Data
Ingalls, Ann.
 Seth and Savannah build a speech / by Ann Ingalls ; illustrated
by Karen Lee.
    p. cm. -- (Writing builders)
 Includes bibliographical references.
 Summary: "Two friends share their stories as they learn how to
create and deliver a speech"--Provided by publisher.
 ISBN-13: 978-1-59953-511-1 (library ed. : alk. paper)
 ISBN-10: 1-59953-511-4 (library ed. : alk. paper)
 ISBN-13: 978-1-60357-391-7 (e-book)
 ISBN-10: 1-60357-391-7 (e-book)
 1. Speechwriting--Juvenile literature. I. Lee, Karen (Karen
Jones), 1961-
ill. II. Title.
 PN4142.I55 2012
 808.5--dc23
                              2011038971

Manufactured in the United States of America in North
Mankato, Minnesota.
195N—012012

Words in **black bold** are defined in the glossary.

Giving a Speech Is Like Riding a Bike!

I am very good at riding a bike. My friend Savannah likes to ride, too. I love to plan bike races with my friends. We decide where to hold a race, check to make sure that place is open, and choose a date and a time. We make signs to advertise the race and to mark the starting and finish lines.

I was nervous when I found out I had to give a two-minute speech for school, but Savannah told me that giving a speech is a lot like racing a bike. The introduction is the starting line. The key points are check points in a race. The conclusion is a finish line.

I totally understood how she explained it! I'm going to glide through that speech like I would glide over the finish line—just two minutes start to finish!

By Seth, age 10

When Seth hopped on his bike for his ride home from school, Savannah called out, "Seth! Wait up!"

She ran up, snapped on her helmet, and jumped on her bike. The two peddled toward Seth's house together.

"What do you think about the speeches we have to give? I'm already almost done with mine," she said. Their teacher, Mr. Endicott, assigned their class to give speeches the next day. They had to fill out worksheets with the main points of their speeches, too.

"Big problem," Seth said, looking worried.

"Come on, Seth. You can do it," she said. "Our speeches can be on any **topic**. Why don't you give one on bike races? You know a lot about that. Actually, a bike race is kind of like a speech."

"How is a bike race like a speech?" Seth asked.

"Well, for one thing, you have to plan it," said Savannah. "You have to decide what you're going to talk about. Do you want to teach something, **persuade** people to do something, or make them laugh?"

"I know I could make them laugh," Seth said. He looked over his shoulder at Savannah and made a goofy face.

"That's not what I mean," laughed Savannah.

When Seth and Savannah got to Seth's house, they told Seth's grandpa, Mr. Boscombe, about their class assignment and the worksheets they had to fill out.

"I'm sure you can do that, Seth," said Mr. Boscombe. "Have you got any ideas?"

"Yes, a bunch!" said Seth. "But I don't know how to start."

Savannah opened her backpack and pulled out a stack of index cards. "First, you need a lot of index cards. When you give a speech, you don't read the whole thing. You read notes from index cards."

"Okay," said Seth. "But what do I write on them?"

Savannah grabbed her speech worksheet from her backpack and handed it to Mr. Boscombe. "I already started filling out the parts of the speech," she smiled.

9

Mr. Boscombe smoothed out the worksheet on the table. He pointed to the paper and explained, "A speech has three main parts: an introduction, key points, and a conclusion."

Seth read aloud from the worksheet. "Introduction: A summary of the points you want to get across."

"An introduction has to be interesting," added Savannah, "to the point and not too long."

"That's right," said Mr. Boscombe. "You want to get everyone's attention. Think about what your **audience** might want to know."

"Now, read this," said Savannah.

Introduction:
My speech is about jumping rope. My friends and I jump rope on the playground every day. We have lots of fun and learn new skipping moves and rhymes. Maybe you'd like to try this.

"I get it!" said Seth. "I'll start by telling everyone how much fun bike races are."

"The next thing you have to do is decide on the key points, what you want to say about your topic," said Mr. Boscombe.

They all looked at Savannah's worksheet again.

Key Points:
Jumping rope is good exercise.
It's a good way to have fun with your friends.
You can make up jump rope rhymes of your own.

"Each of your key points can have several **subpoints**," Mr. Boscombe said.

"Now Seth, you decide what the key points of your speech will be," said Savannah.

"Remember you shouldn't write down everything you want to say," added Mr. Boscombe. "Just enough to remind you of your main ideas. Your speech will sound better if you're talking, not reading."

"Okay," said Seth. He started to write his ideas on the note cards, one on each card. Then Seth showed Savannah what he had written:

race officials

prizes

get help planning from friends

signs for the start of the race and for the finish

drinks for thirsty racers

find a place

check points

contact the park

plotting race course

bathroom breaks

when to pass
in a bike race

wearing helmets

15

"I can't use all of these," said Seth. "I can't keep them straight."

"You do have a big stack of cards," said Savannah. "Just choose the most important things to tell about."

Seth placed some of the cards to one side and kept the others in his stack to talk about. He kept cards that said:

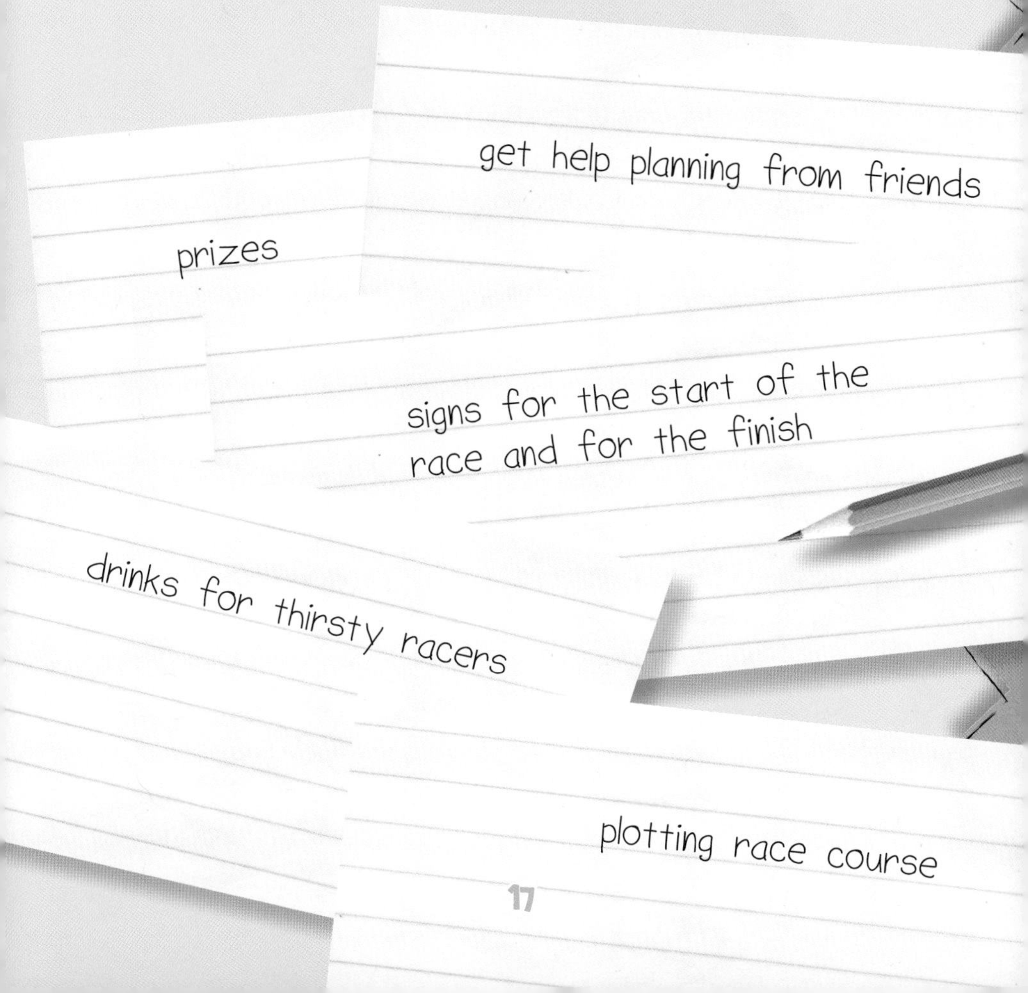

get help planning from friends

prizes

signs for the start of the race and for the finish

drinks for thirsty racers

plotting race course

"This is great," said Savannah. "Now what do you want to tell them about each key point?"

"I'll work on that," said Seth.

He grabbed more note cards and wrote a few words on each one telling a bit more about each key point. He put similar points together and wrote some new points.

"Then you just decide what order you want the cards to follow," added Savannah. "I wrote a number in the corner of each card so if I drop them I can put them back in order."

Seth set his note cards out in order.

1

get help planning from friends
meet with friends
pick a time and place
contact the park

2

signs for the start of the
race and for the finish
plotting race course

3

prizes

4

drinks for thirsty racers
check points

5

18 people came
plan for next year

"The very last thing you have to do is to come up with your conclusion," said Savannah. She read from the worksheet, "Conclusion: It should sum up all of your key points and remind everyone what you just talked about."

"I know!" said Seth. "I'll end with how fun bike racing is!"

Seth and Savannah worked for a long time. Mr. Boscombe brought each of them a nice tall glass of lemonade.

"Are you ready to practice your speeches?" asked Mr. Boscombe. "Practicing will make you more comfortable with your speech. You'll do a better job when you go in front of your audience. Try not to read from your note cards. Just glance at them."

"I'll go first," volunteered Savannah.

Mr. Boscombe said, "Remember to speak loudly enough so the people in the back of the room can hear you."

Savannah stood up tall, straightened her shoulders, and began, "Today I'm going to talk about jumping rope."

She went all the way through the speech, flipping one card after another until she got to the very last one. She stopped twice but just for a few seconds. When she was done, Savannah gave Mr. Boscombe and Seth a big smile. Seth gave Savannah a thumbs up.

"Nice job!" said Mr. Boscombe. "I learned a lot about jumping rope that I never knew before."

"You hardly stopped at all," added Seth. "Your index cards really worked!"

"Thanks, Seth!" replied Savannah. "Now it's your turn."

Seth gulped the last bit of his lemonade and began. He started with his introduction. He spoke from memory.

"Have you ever ridden in a bike race? You get to go really fast, and sometimes you even win! But planning a bike race can be just as much fun."

Then, he looked at his first note card. He said:

"The first thing you want to do is to get some friends to help with planning. Planning a bike race is too much work for one person. Besides, it's lots more fun to work together.

"Have a meeting with your friends and decide when and where you want to have the race. We had our first race at Levagood Park.

"My mom and I called the park service people. They said we could have the race on the first Sunday in June. The weather was just right."

Seth smiled as he went on to the next note card. With each point, he felt more comfortable. When he didn't know what to say next, the note card reminded him.

At last, he finished his main points. He said his conclusion:

"Finally, I would like to say that riding a bike is great exercise and is loads of fun. My friends and I plan our own bike races. We even draw our own maps. Bike races take lots of planning, but they are worth all the trouble. Nothing beats a bike race on a good sunny day."

When Seth was all done, he grinned. "I have to admit, Savannah, you were right. Giving a speech is like a bike race. It takes planning, but it's worth it and it's a lot of fun!"

You Can Give a Speech, Too!

Would you like to give a speech? There are three good reasons to do this: You can inform people, you can persuade people, or you can entertain people.

Three Parts of a Speech

A speech has three parts: the introduction, the key points (or the body of the speech), and the conclusion.

The introduction tells your audience what the speech is about. The key points are the ideas you want to share. In the conclusion, you sum up the ideas in your speech.

Preparing to Write

Write down some ideas about what you want to talk about before you give your speech. Write your ideas on note cards. Then choose which ideas you want to share in your speech.

Writing the Speech

Add subpoints to the ideas on each note card. Don't write down every word you want to say. Just write enough to remind you of your idea. Decide in what order the note cards should go and number the corner of each card.

Giving Your Speech

When you give your speech, imagine that you are talking to your family or friends. Practice in front of family or friends or in front of a mirror. That way, you will be more relaxed. At the end of your speech, be prepared for questions. If you don't know the answers to a question, it's all right to say so. You can always find out the answer and get back to people.

Glossary

audience: the people who listen to a speech or other performance.

persuade: to explain your ideas to get someone to agree with you.

subpoints: ideas that support one of the main ideas.

topic: the main subject or idea.

For More Information

Books

Juskow, Barbara. *Speakers' Club: Public Speaking for Young People*. Waco, TX: Prufrock Press, 2005.

O'Neal, Katherine Pebley. *Public Speaking: 7 Steps To Writing And Delivering A Great Speech*. Waco, TX: Prufrock Press, 2005.

Websites

Interesting Speech Topics for Kids
http://www.buzzle.com/articles/interesting-speech-topics-for-kids.html
This website lists kid-friendly ideas for speech topics.

Speech Tips
http://www.speechtips.com/
This website gives detailed information about planning, writing, and giving speeches.

About the Author

Ann Ingalls has written more than 100 stories and poems for children of all ages as well as resource materials for parents and teachers. When she isn't writing she enjoys spending time with her family and friends, traveling, reading, knitting, and playing with her cats.